The Throb of Silence

Thamizhachi Thangapandian

Translation from Tamil
K S Subramanian

Vitasta

Published by
Renu Kaul Verma
Vitasta Publishing Pvt Ltd
2/15, Ansari Road, Daryaganj
New Delhi-110 002
info@vitastapublishing.com

ISBN 978-93-90961-65-8

First Edition 2023

MRP ₹425

This Poetry collection is entirely a work of fiction. Names, characters, events and incidents are entirely imaginary. Reference to real places, actual regions, institutions or community practices has been made in a fictitious manner. Any resemblance to actual persons, living or dead or actual events is purely coincidental.

Special Thanks: Latha Ramakrishnan

'Wrapper Art by Vallabhai'
Illustrations by P Manivannan
Editorial Support by Alisha Verma
Cover and layout by Somesh Kumar Mishra
Printed by Chaman Enterprises, Delhi

CONTENTS

'Thamizhachi's poetry is...' — *vii*

'In her prose and poetry...' — *xxiii*

Golden Beetle In Matchbox — 1

The Bus And A Few Mynahs — 3

The Voyage — 6

The Search — 8

The Beginning — 10

My Pongal — 13

Inside, Outside — 15

My Poetry — 17

Neem Flower In Summer — 19

The Sixth Sense — 21

Creeping Darkness — 24

Chencholai	25
Passing On	28
Vanappechi	29
A Sharing	32
Confrontation	34
Al Janabi's Sixth Finger	37
Eve's Drop	39
Torture	42
Our Chemistry	44
To That Vulture	46
The Forest Kiss	48
Alone....	51
Lost	52
The Riddle	55
Growth	57
Stumbling	60
A Shell	62
Aridity, A Ballad	65
The Manjanathi Tree	68

The Forest Smouldered And Died Down 73

Rain And Rain-Laden Life 77

Date With Rain 78

The Taste Of Sun 79

The Little Girl And Her Fallen Teeth 81

Untitled 85

Musical Chair 88

Blessing 91

Generation 95

It Was Sunset Time 99

An Encounter 103

Arugan 106

My Death 109

What? 113

The Other Side 115

The Shadow 118

To Each Unto Herself 120

Handshake And Loudspeakers 124

The Throb Of Silence 125
Ode To Software 127
Greeting Morrow 128
A New Angle 131
Genital Blood 133
Untitled 137
Evolutionary Change 138
Hope Enduring 141
Rain Finds Its Level 142
From Appa To Appa 144
Not Much, O Worthies! 145
Defeat 149
The Great Arrival 151

Glossary *153*
About The Translator *157*

'Thamizhachi's poetry is unique and distinctive. She brings the heft of her personality to her art, which makes her work poignant, reflective and thought-provoking.'

—N Kalyan Raman
Literary Translator

The tradition of classical Tamil poetry is nearly 2000 years old. However, with the advent of modernity set in motion by the colonial period, change was inevitable in all aspects of Tamil life, including the practice of art and literature. 'Puthukkavithai,' or 'new poetry,' a genre that broke free of the constraints of traditional poetry – such as metre and rhyme – and aspired to be a mode of expression for the full range of the modern imagination, was born ninety years ago. Though it remained the province of the 'literate' upper castes initially, the Puthukkavithai movement has gathered a steady stream of new adherents over the decades – workers, peasants, Dalits, women and enthusiasts of every description from a rapidly expanding middle class.

However, the number of women participating in literary production has been relatively low. For the poet, poetry is a mode of expression that is deeply personal and intimate. Given our age-old patriarchal culture, women have had to fight to create spaces for such expression, and then to be acknowledged with respect. Despite these challenges, many brilliant and robust voices have emerged to create a rich corpus of contemporary women's poetry in Tamil. They have covered a wide range of themes and written eloquently from a woman's point of view on life, love, and this world in which we make our lives.

Dr. T Sumathy (aka) Thamizhachi Thangapandian, the author of this collection, has made her mark as a distinctive poetic voice over the past twenty years. Having pursued a distinguished career as a teacher and scholar of literature, she is making a significant contribution to society as a politician in her capacity as Member of Parliament representing an important constituency in Chennai. Thamizhachi has published five collections of poetry to wide critical attention and acclaim in the Tamil milieu. *Internal Colloquies*, a collection of her poems in English (translated with an introduction by eminent translator, CT Indra) appeared in 2019. The present work is the second collection of her poetry in translation.

In an age where tempers run high and abstraction holds sway over our consciousness, Thamizhachi's perspective is poised and rooted, paying close attention not only to the natural world but also to the tremors of the passing moment in herself and others. Her voice is gentle and reflective, steeped in irony and wonder at the ways of the world, and sensitive to her own fears and yearnings.

In what seems like a poet's manifesto (*My Poetry*), Tamizhachi carves out a space where she is free to be herself without the need to follow conventions or participate in any 'festival.' In a sense, it is the nature of her poetry – 'unclothed and guileless.'

A time past
of flawless grammar
and flowing rhythm
The present
steeped in
semiotic strategies
modern and postmodern fiction
deconstruction and sundry 'isms'
In the melee of this festival
my poetry has
happily lost its way
like an unclothed, guileless child

A recurring theme in Thamizhachi's poems is the nuance of the moment, in which the human stakes are always high. The chasm between two people is portrayed delicately in *The Beginning*:

Drawing a fine
imperceptible screen
between us, we read –
with the air of a weaver
carefully examining
thin strands of thread –
the lines on our palms, growing
heavy of heart and weary as well

The same sense of gloom and resignation about relationships is expressed in *Me and You*:

Just as a tear dwells
inside every
rebuffed smile
all is contained
In every meeting of ours
Our meetings take place
like a drongo taking flight
with the breathless gasp
of a closely threaded
string of flowers –
alive and singed

every time, like a bird
in a painting flapping its wings.

In *Shade,* the poet comes to realise that the pain of a severed friendship hurts both equally and in such moments of epiphany lies the power to heal oneself. In *Defeat,* the poet's own craft is subject to the vagaries of the moment:

The pen,
unsheathed
with the ferocity
of a bloodhound,
is lidded shut
like the feeble whimper
of an old, ailing woman
sometimes
when poetry
sediments as silt
between
the heat of emotion
and the filter of words

As someone born in a village with a living connection to her native place, to the community and their way of life, the poet often feels dissonance in the urban environment, in the sameness of human experience shared with the faceless crowd. But the memory of what she has left behind offers succour and refuge, and more vitally, keeps her imagination alive.

In the first poem in this collection, *Golden Beetle in a Matchbox*, Thamizhachi's coda to her litany of disappointments is taking comfort in nostalgic memories of the past:

> Turning
> deaf in the din of buses
> dyspeptic from watching television
> faceless among digital images
> crippled from living in cocoons
> I lost my way in the city
> but to wake me up at midnight
> make me laugh and help me
> find myself again

I hold on to the memory
of my native village
like the golden beetle
I had treasured
in a matchbox as a child

In another poem, *A Bus and a Few Mynahs*, she compares the freedom of mynahs to the condition of an urban woman travelling in a bus, surrounded and harassed by a faceless crowd:

Mynahs have vast playgrounds
and sprawling meadows to inhabit
If they want, they are free
to eat
gaze upward at the sky
dig up the dirt and bury their face in it
if idle, push their beak into the wings
mate with a partner
else, kick up a row
and if none of these are possible
even pass away in peace

Most of the poems in this collection are about the exigencies of modern life and the human condition, particularly from a woman's perspective. *The Voyage* is about migrants to a foreign land. The poet sees beyond the romantic notion of extending your horizons to the psychological and material reality of migration.

> We renounced the native soil
> forgot the paths traversed
> felt the fury of gales
> and squally rain
> inner and outer selves adrift
> on the swirling waters of the ocean
> carrying only the hazy memory
> that endures as a treasure within
> while the body's cordage is rolled up
> and the chariot of life is brought to station
> you are washed ashore in an alien land
> on the soil of a foreign language

The word of trickery, away from the

light, is portrayed in *Darkness*. The poet is at once realistic and sensitive about the world she lives in:

I tell them that electric lights
dazzle my eyes and always
start my mischiefs in the semi-dark
It's right for the pretences and trickeries
lying scattered in the space
before the next step on the ladder
It comes with the benefit of avoiding
the guileless eyes of the other

Benediction, is a delightful poem about how a child entering a new house subverts the meaning and grammar of a conventional household with its spontaneity, and bring a fresh, meditative quality of being in the moment to the staid habits of the adult world. In *Generation*, the poet describes with humour opposite tastes, tendencies and perspectives inhabiting the same individual and the absurdity of identifying the whole with any part thereof. It's reminiscent of Walt Whitman's *I Contain Multitudes*, but instead of the grizzly poet's vehement self-assertion, Thamizhachi gives us her wonder and amusement at the plurality of selves contained in us.

As someone who is close to the ethos of a village, surrounded by a natural world that is intimately intertwined with the community and the residents, Thamizhachi is very sensitive to life as a continuum and her own place between the past and the future, between ancestors and progeny. She gives expression to this sentiment in her marvellous poem, *The Source*:

It's an effort
not to leave anything behind
that may evoke memories
the dampness of sweat
when parting from friends
the spittle of rancour
while facing enemies
the horror of a fake smile
while avoiding traitors
Since even a word to our progeny

must be receive from our ancestors
how could we not leave something behind
that may evoke memories?

In another beautiful poem, *Manjanathi*, (the native name for the Indian mulberry tree that grows in the poet's native region in southern Tamil Nadu), the tree becomes a confidant from the days of innocent childhood through puberty and adulthood to old age. As she says goodbye in the last section, the poet sees Manjanathi as a bridge between her and women of the future.

Manjanathi, my primordial mother!
Even after I turn into an ancient woman
with grey hairs sprouting on my chin
I'll come to lay my head on your lap
Keep my wrinkled old age wrapped
in a dried brown leaf from an ancient tree
Someday a heavily pregnant shepherd lass

will stop by and take away
the flower of life inside.

The Forest is another poignant poem that is a lyrical tribute to the forest as a refuge from the loss, grief and hurts of living, as the final resting place of one's ancestors as much as oneself, but even more organically, as the space that belongs not only to forsaken hatchlings but also to fireflies that glow momentarily and disappear and to butterflies with newly sprouted wings.

A breathtaking description of the palm grove as an erotic space is in the poem, *Wastewater*, with the image of the imp (Pecchi) walking in silence, like the quiet flow of wastewater, not towards gentlemen lusting after wealth but in search of the sickle-wielding ferocity of guardian deities. Thamizhachi's poetry, and her vision, are never far from her roots and the world of imagination they evoke.

The early decades of the present

century have been filled with war, violence and genocide. Thamizhachi's poem on the Sri Lankan army's attack on an orphanage in *Sencholai*, is an expression of clear-eyed anguish and heart-breaking imagery.

> Anything was possible
> on that pathway
> The morning had dawned with
> with the promise of kisses
> On that day too, the bird was sitting on that tree
> Counting on the certain prospect of a smile
> The staircase, too, was waiting
> to pass minutes as if they were moments
> The playground around the flagmast
> awash in the silence of prayer
> Those bedsheets had stashed
> a final stretch to shake off drowsiness
> Abnormally,
> a child's severed hand that fell
> on the football was holding
> an uneaten morsel of breakfast

> The path had indeed been pregnant
> with all kinds of dreams.

One of the central motifs in Thamizhachi's poetry is the female imp who roams the forest. The imps – Pecchis – are beyond the conventional expectations of feminine behaviour. They live on their own, protective of women everywhere and combative in their ethereal presence. In 'Foetal Blood,' the poet weaves into the narrative of the poem the response of the Pecchis to the horrific incidents of gangrape and violence against women that happened recently in the country. It's a way of evoking the primordial to raise a cry for justice for women in the contemporary world. *To Each Unto Herself* is the Pecchis' anger and grief at the rape and genocide of young Tamil girls in Eelam. There are poems in this collection where the Pecchis deal with the more of city life.

Not only in its themes and concerns but also in its poetic vision, Thamizhachi's poetry is unique and distinctive. A remarkable degree of maturity and poise is evident in her response to the world and to her own personal predicaments. She brings the heft of her personality to her art, which makes her work poignant, reflective and thought-provoking. If Puthukkavithai in Tamil is still a new and growing country, Thamizhachi can be counted among its gifted and brave ambassadors.

* *The translation of the poems in the foreword has been done by N Kalyan Raman.*

'In her prose and poetry, Thamizhachi is struggling to keep alive and celebrate pristine feminine power which has been time and again trampled by successive phases of urbanisation and modernisation presided over by patriarchy.'

—H S Shivaprakash
Poet, Playwright and Translator

Thamizhachi's Poetry as Rite of Passage

How come a lovely butterfly baby
came out of an ugly moth?
How to solve
the riddle of beauty?

****

In the valour of fire
forest smoldered and died down.
Even after this catastrophe

O which no quicksand of History
can gulp down
I had to eat the next meal!

The two quotes above sum up in a gnomic way the dilemmas of the word and the world. They are explored in the unique poetry of Thamizhachi, translated and included in this volume.

What happens to poetry, which though, composed by individual poets, speaks of the collective, when historical epochs change violently? The throes that the collective experiences, the poets not only experience more acutely but express memorably. It is thus, that poetry becomes a rite of passage, a bridge over the troubled waves of times or a word-ark where our troubled selves can rest, recuperate and regain strength to face, to steal a phrase from my favourite philosopher AN Whitehead, 'the hard and irreducible facts of experience.' Poetry-writing—non-poets hardly do it, normal ones do it—unconsciously, half-heartedly.

But true poets take the bull by the horn and plunge their vessel into the heart of the storm and come back intact to set us an example of how to brave the challenge and survive even when one cannot succeed.

That is why the greatest poetry comes into being in moments of violent crisis and transition. In such periods of churning, what is at stake is the eikos of the poet's community—that space where we grow, cohabit, live, labour and eventually die, leaving behind the posterity. The churning maybe on account of a human or natural calamity: floods, famines, volcanic eruptions, spread of pandemics, wars, revolutions or genocides.

These are not everyday events but more or less, a constant source of predicaments during historical paradigm shifts. One of the most life-transforming upheavals whose seismic effect is felt profoundly in poetry everywhere is the crushing impact of the modern city. This great disruption, though nearly two centuries old, still effects in different degrees in poetry. Even though the process of dehumanisation, as a result of the rise of the imperialist city, has a universal pattern, its regional manifestation varies from place to place, language to language.

The foregoing observations were necessary to situate the poetry of Thamizhachi, which has a more far reaching significance than understood. In her prose and poetry, she is struggling to keep alive and celebrate pristine feminine power which has been time and again trampled by successive phases of urbanisation and modernisation presided over by patriarchy. The name Thamizhachi identifies this power with is Vanapechi. Who is she?

Let us listen to the poet herself speak about her:

Vanapechi is my Alter Ego

She is an indigenous village deity whose name literally means "a mad, fierce woman who resides in forest." A woman without any shackles, representing the rugged and raw sensibility of a southern regional rural woman!

She never wants any shelter above her head—she's an epitome of free spirit!

She dwells in the forest and resonates the *Matriarchal Supremacy* of Womanhood.

She is people's guardian deity, synonymous with காவல் காப்பதூ in Tamil.

"Through her, I express the untold stories of my women folk, the taboos they want to undo, demystifying those cultural burdens which they are forced to carry on for centuries! She is the Voice of my soul - my partner in crime - my chum - my backup as a pillar of strength!

She is ME!"

Empowered with the surviving spirit of this primeval force, Thamizhachi's poems address the present. Vanapechi herself is not part of dead past though her kind of world is dying. She outlives the corrosion of her natural habitat, enters and interacts with the modern world because she is still alive deep in the poet's being and voice. Her dealings with the new world and its lifeless order is essentially tragi-comical but also, absurd and amusing as written in *Vanappechi*.

In which house in the packed city
where tensions hide,
like a serpent, coiled in deceptive quiet
can we find
the cradle cloth for an infant
and the string pouch for the elderly?
This a great worry
for Vanappechi, Lady of Woods
Shouldn't be sitting at the dining table
stroking the hip mark
Shouldn't be shaking
the dark calf muscles....
With considerable preparation
I had assembled friends
in that house for chat,
but no place
for warm togetherness
Not finding a safe nook
for spouting a volley of betel juice

She liked only the Gorkha at the gate
for his beedi and security

Her concern is not with the orderliness of the spick and span posh house. She is worried about the comfort of the baby and the elderly. Because that is no place for the vulnerable or for spouting beetle juice, Vanapechi is not at home in this house but with the Gorkha who too is an exile and outsider like her.

In another poem, Vanapechi ventures into the city with her attendant deities. They return with the bounty of sanitary napkins and birth control tablets, both of which are antonyms of primeval and uninhibited fertility of Vanapechi. Though her bundles are bursting with meat balls giving the aroma of the whole city, she is at a loss as to how she should satisfy the demands of seven virgins. The poet further writes:

Impeccable grammar

the plethora of metre

contrived symbols
modernist, post-modernist frames
deconstruction and other -isms
How good
in the ongoing sacred festival
my poetry lost its way
and turned naked
like a baby*

This meta-poetic poem is the manifesto of Thamizhachi's poems. It declares its independence from both classical Tamil tradition and from modernist and post-modernist models. Her poetry has turned 'naked like baby.'

The metaphor of nakedness of a baby is extremely compelling. The nude baby is not all new for it carries ancestral impressions in body and mind. It is a link between the dead, the living and the unborn. All genuine poetry is the exploration of the self which cannot be divorced from ancestors.

The poetic self is, after all a link between ancestors and successors through us. Thamizhachi is keenly aware of it:

> While passing on even one word
> from ancestors
> how can we help
> passing on to successors
> something worth treasuring?

Apart from kinship with ancestors, there is another source of strength in Thamizhachi's poetry—what Yeats would call 'that true contact with the earth/ From which everything Aeneas-like grows,' in her connectedness to the landscape of her childhood, the second womb where she grew up, that Thamizhachi relates herself the concept of *tinai* in ancient Tamil poetry and poetics. This does not mean she is repeating the practice of ancient Tamil poets because she does not go back to 5 *tinais* of ancient poets. Through her familiarity, she has imbibed the essence of her belongingness to the landscape of her village which she invokes through the image of specific and compelling Manjanathi tree, which is at the heart of this landscape, means more to her than her own kith and kin.

New spreading pallor,
lost friendships....
Manjanathi tree!
At the mid-day hour
You are languorous
with leaves frozen still
The pain of betrayal
Is borne by your blunted thorns.
Your flowers laden with toddy
are my heady secrets
Your fruits dripping with honey
know the savour of my longings.
My primeval mother, Manjanathi!
Even after I turn a grand mother
stray grey sprouting of my chin
I would seek you out
to snuggle in your lap.
Then
secure my shrivelled old age

in a parched leaf.
Some day I would tarry and take away
the life-flower inside
like a very pregnant shepherdess.

What a far cry from the usual run of alienated nature poetry! Here the tree is almost like the extension of the speaker's body and mind. The poems included in this volume, though held together by leitmotifs of human and nature's fertility, address a variety of themes and situations in the absurdity of the present.

The basic contradiction is not only between innate order of the poet's inherited past and artificiality of imposed urban modernity but also between all-embracing feminine instinct and limit-setting man's power dramatised in poems about man-woman relationship. This relationship is not a matter just between members of two different genders, but a union which constitutes seamless continuity with ancestry and environment:

Between you and me
there is only the sea
One salty teardrop of yours
settles on the shore as the sliver of foam.
The moon above
is your Amma's frozen breastmilk;
The the sea waves,
your father's good night kisses;
and darting crabs,
your friendly playmates

In another poem:

A drop of rain dripping into the house
and clearing the muck of the morning;
mother's bosom
pulsating with plentiful milk;
When dream grabs the moments
tailed by memory
it is the weightless bodies

When this man-woman-nature-ancestry connect is lacking, it leads to conception of question marks instead of a human foetus. This nightmare is shockingly depicted Kafka-like in the poem. About how to confront the world of question mark there is an unsettled debate in the mind of woman, now split up into three voices:

For her,
language is prayer.
For me
the breath of life
determined by feelings and needs.
For the third
the sound of ribaldry
All born, traversed and merged
In this ocean
which drop is mine?

The asymmetry between nature and culture, feminine and masculine, the spontaneous and the spurious is replicated in poems on (wo)man and machine:

The 'beep' sounds announce

the short messages
The notes exchanged all night
stay wiped out in your chat realm
and the moisture of kisses
have dried up
Your inbox brimming with
smile-likes and thanks
Like a stallion itching for the race,
your cell phone.
With so many 'soft' notes
eagerly lingering
how come you're still asleep,
O Software girl

Beneath this surface of absurdity and contradiction, sometimes sad and amusing, there is the rotten underbelly of rape and violence against woman-nature which is powerfully dramatised in the following and a few other similar poems:

That path was meant
all kinds of possibilities.
That morning dawned

with assurances for kisses
Smiles on singled out
For the bird perching
on the branch of the tree
beneath which awaited stone steps
to rush minutes into moments;
the flagmast ground
soaked in stifled prayers;
those bedspreads
shrouding themselves in
the parting yawn of indolence
Unusually on that football
lay the severed hand of a baby
holding remnants of
the morning food
And numberless dreams
stretched that path.
(Chencholai)

In the world fraught with unresolved conflicts and contradictions, violence and terror consequent upon the disruption of holistic values of tribal and rural communities—the world of Vanapechi-

stemming from the seamless continuity of human kinship with ancestors and posterity, on the one hand, and with environment where we cohabit the planet alongside other living and non-living occupants, is not a lost hope or a sweet memory. In spite of being disrupted violently it is still a remote possibility, which is already a reality made manifest in moments of Thamizhachi's poetic epiphanies:

> You observe only the
> spoken word
> ignoring with disdain
> the language
> of the eyes, earlobes and fingers
> Do you at all know
> the pumpkin flower
> planted in the Markazhi kolam
> in the opposite yard
> is a heart!

I have only tried here to identify and talk about the major strands in Thamizhachi's poetry. There is a great deal to say about several remarkable individual poems in the volume though I have a feeling that translation, in general, interferes with our appreciation. But I hope that I have pointed out the uniqueness of her poetry. She is attempting what no other contemporary poet I know of seems to be doing. Her deeply nuanced poems see the disruption of a lifestyle based on the unity and harmony of the human, animal, plant and the non-living and feminine and matriarchal values uncensored by patriarchal oppression is at the root of the absurdity, dissonance and frequent outbursts of destructive violence in the world we live in. It is in one sense the critique of technological progress at the expense of life principle.

Unlike a lot of such critiques, however, her poems do not invoke the past in terms of the naïveté and innocence. The beings, human and quasi-human, who dwell and animate the *tinai* of her poetry are full of life-asserting values: passion, playfulness, spontaneity and compassion.

Unlike most contemporary poets Thamizhachi does not perceive the crisis of our age from the alienated perspectives of adherents of present-day ideologies imported from outside or with the uncritical view of blind nativism. True, she bemoans 'the ugly tide of modernism,' but she suggests the possibility, however remote, of recovery and renewal not through appeal to eternally deferred utopia of the past or future but through the passionate questioning of the here and now.

* ***The translation of the poem has been done by Shivaprakash***

To my bundles
of joy
Aadhira & Adhiyan

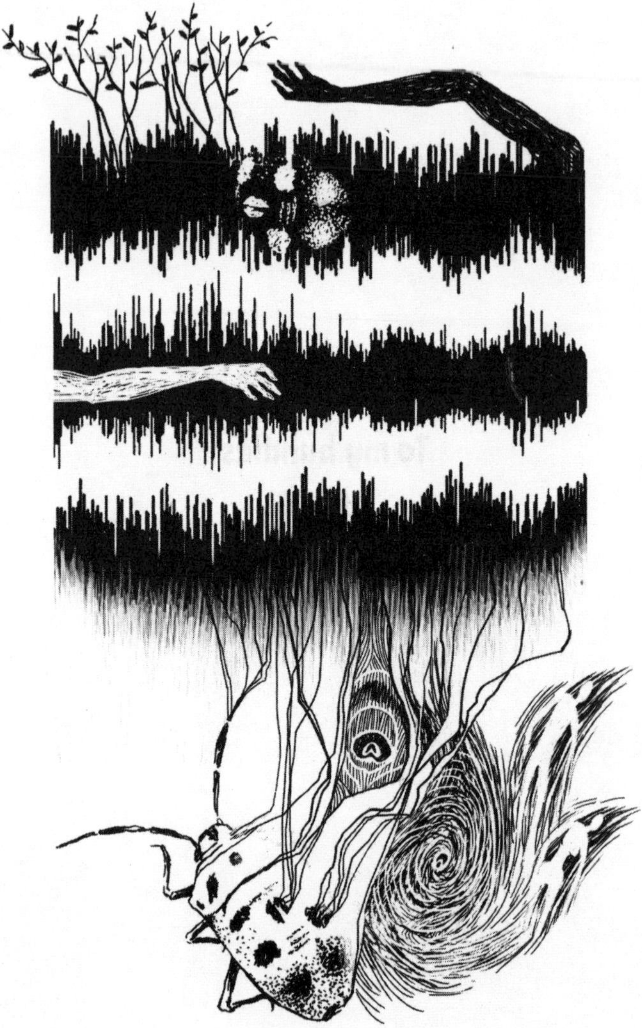

GOLDEN BEETLE IN MATCHBOX

Pre-dawn sleep:
time to be stirred
by the sight the sky

Since the first day in the city
after leaving the hamlet far away
the windows have been shut tight
blacking out the neighbor next door,
How lifeless the blinds!
—a curse for ever

The twilight descends
as the dissolving rays
greet the peacock's homesteads
near the inviting fields....

Here
at the stroke of five
the netted windows
warding off mosquitoes are shut

—a hasty meaningless ritual

The relatives in the kitchen
serving any and everything
are all from homes close by
—nameless strangers
From the layers of wall-eggs
emerge many anaemic faces

Deafened by the din of the bus
forced by TV boxes
the face lost in the myriad computer
forms,
crippled in a cocooned life….
I am all lost in the city

In the midnight
slumber tickles me
into the memory of my hamlet

—the golden beetle
I have treasured
in a tiny matchbox
I collected when small

THE BUS AND A FEW MYNAHS

For the Myna
a vast space and an expansive lawn
mean one and the same

When they feel like
They peck at tiny insects
and taste the feast,
can gaze at the captivating sky
burrow in the ground
and bury the face

When exhausted
they can snuggle the beak
into their cozy wings,
can mate in bliss
with a loving partner

Or else,
they can hop their way to sacred

solitude
can live without their own home

If all else slips away
they quietly meet their end

Better, all this, than
Being a girl
getting squeezed
in a crowded bus

Avoiding the pounding forearms
and wrapping tight the 'pallu' of the
sari
Getting down from the bus,
I have a doubt:
Are all the mynahs I see
but only men?

THE VOYAGE

Abandoning the birthplace
forgetting the trodden paths
feeling the fury of the lashing gale
losing identity
in the churning waves
carrying only a shadowy memory
buried deep inside
the fatigued lifeline
crushed and crumbled
on the life-chariot

Washed on to a foreign shore
amidst the medley of an alien tongue

Like orphaned shells no one
cares to pick up,
like salted meat
with no trace of blood

clasping to the chest

a passport of trepidation

Carrying the hapless refugees
The ship adrift
spat out
in some distant port
in some corner of the globe
a cargo of salty life

THE SEARCH

Of these rail carriages
of anonymous likeness
which is this door
I don't know

Still
during all journeys
every time
my mind harks back
to the far off day
when I,
pregnant and too weary
to stand for long,
exhausted like a slender lotus stalk
weighed down by burden of
pregnancy,
was on the road

Trying to change into a dress
more comfortable to sleep in,

unsteady, I could totter and tumble

With this fear deep within
with the care and concern of a sculptor
deftly handling the chisel
While driving a hole in the stone
without hurting the fingers

my dear Appa with so much of Amma
in him
held that door a little ajar....

I keep searching till day
To discover
if this door
is the same as that one far away

THE BEGINNING

Keeping vigil in silence
the Word watches fun
conveniently dangling
between the two of us

With the mien of a weaver
intently examining
the strands of thread in the loom
holding a near invisible
gossamer screen
we both heavy with attention
holding each other's palms.

Neither a single angry syllable,
nor forlorn sighs,
not a streak of grouse on the face,
only the clock-hand
holds sway over this room.

I wait for the moment

for one of us
to break the frost of the room
with the warmth of even a tiny cough,
carrying only the clock-hand
never used to waiting.

MY PONGAL

Sweeping the yard clean,
drawing the rice-flour kolam,
placing the bronze pot on a clay oven
painted with ochre stripes,
pouring milk into the pot,
adding jiggery lumps and cashews
applying a liberal dose of ghee
and taking the pot down….

With the harvest failing,
Pongal made with the rice from the
store
leaves but a trifle bitter.

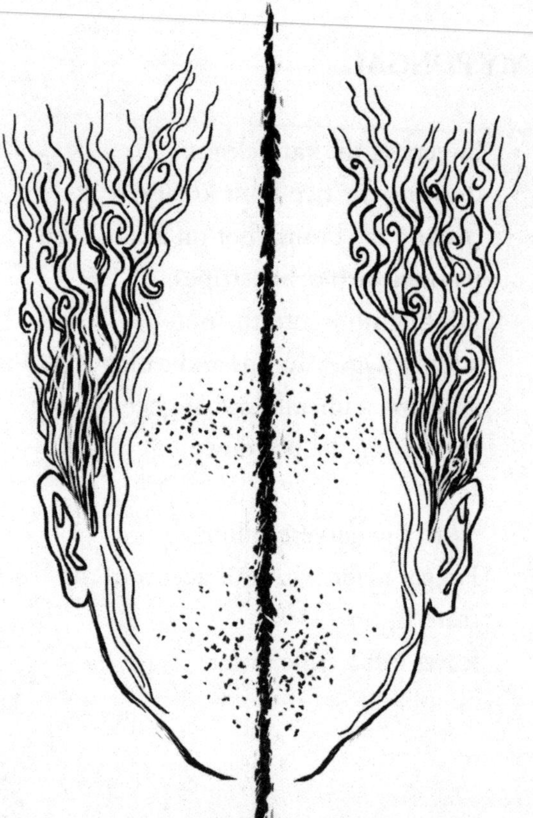

INSIDE, OUTSIDE

Unable to dissolve and drink up
the dark sky
unable to contain indigestion,
the sea spews froth

As stubborn waves ask:
'Coming the night after?'
The moon slips away

Splashing and washing faces
with salt water
combing the hair with cold wind,
the boats are making themselves up
looking into flag pole mirrors

My home, my village Narippaiyur
woke up languorously from slumber
to soil the lovely sun
dipped in the evening

and rising with handful of pearls
in the moon.

Appa's ashes
immersed in the waters
of the sea near my village
as if reversing the alphabet,
On this seashore alone

MY POETRY

A phrase of precision
glowing in perfect prosody
impeccable grammar
rules of metaphors;

An innovative phrase,
Modern, Post Modernist
or deconstructionist;

Good
my verse wandered far afield
from both
and turned naked
like a baby

NEEM FLOWER IN SUMMER

Fed on the intensity
of summer heat
the village
in the grip
of unbearable indigestion

Rinsing the mouth
in cool rain water
spring
is just a rumor
in the orphaned Chembu

Even cooking water
is teasingly salty

The village tank is a reminder
the size of a palm

The village Kanmaai tank
wriggles as a centipede

parched and crumbled

Your longing memory
lingering like a peacock feather
buried in the dried up Kanmaai
bed….

As the memory coalesced into a dark
cloud
a cruel wind tears it apart
as if only tears are the proper rain
for this wretched black soil.

THE SIXTH SENSE

At the door of midnight...
The sound of your feeble sobs
crosses the door
slams my sterile ears
breaks asunder
and dabs the walls
Unable to stand the futile sob
I close my eyes somewhat

Your tremulous sobs
rip open my eyes
and seep in flaming vitriol

Your love escapes with struggle
—a charred stench
my nose smells
as the stench of undigested breastmilk

What do I need to give you
for your friendship and warmth?

When retreating with dismay
Like a beggar woman ruthlessly driven
away
What else do I have
except my black-hued tears
and the love lingering
like the sixth sense!

CREEPING DARKNESS

Blaming the blinding glare of bright
lamps,
my mischiefs set off
only in semi-darkness
—a convenient prelude
to the exploits and hanky-panky
inviting and scattered in the next stage

There is an added benefit:
avoiding the childlike eyes
of the other person
strangle the occasional feelings of guilt

To sharpen the blades of treachery
the burning malice of my eyes
should do

My lies
glow and glitter
in total darkness.

CHENCHOLAI

That path held
all kinds of possibilities.

The morning dawned
with assurances for kisses and smiles
singled out
for the bird perching
on the tree branch
beneath which awaited
stone steps
to rush minutes into moments

The flag mast ground
soaked in stifled prayers;
those bedspreads
shrouding themselves in
the parting yawn of indolence

On that football
lay the severed hand of a baby

holding remnants of
the morning food

Numberless Dreams
Stretched out on the same path

* *When the Sri Lankan army attacked a refuge of orphan children in a place called Chencholai, a large number of children got killed.*

PASSING ON

It takes real hard work
not to leave behind
anything worth remembering

When we part with friends,
the stickiness of sweat;
while encountering foes,
the spit of malice;
while avoiding traitors,
the cruelty of smiles…

While passing on even one word
from ancestors
how can we help
passing on to successors
something worth treasuring?

VANAPPECHI

In which house in the packed city
can we find
the cradle cloth for an infant
and the string pouch for the elderly?

Tensions hide in those houses
like a serpent,
coiled in deceptive hush

This, a great worry
for Vanappechi, Lady of Woods

Don't sit at the dining table
Don't stroke the hip mark
Don't shake
the dark calf muscles....

With considerable preparation
I had assembled friends
in the house for chat,

but no place was there
for warm togetherness

Not finding a safe nook
for spouting a volley of betel juice

She liked only the Goorkha at the gate
for his beedi and security

A SHARING

Till that moment
on that defining day
such a journey
must clearly have been
beyond the understanding
of the jackfruit

Before declaring aloud
the blossoming of its fondness
it was bundled off into the city
and arrived with a wrapping of green
love
for all the houses in that settlement

As an expression
of the goodwill of world leaders
only pets such as Panda, elephant cub,
lion-tailed monkey and the like
filled the list of gifts
hopping inter-continental distances

The modest jackfruit
with its simple sweetness
cannot join the proud list
of those plane-hopping greats

How can one share it lovingly
with totally unfamiliar neighbours?

CONFRONTATION

When you decide
what words I should choose
the silence I keep is strong and
eloquent

When you walk with the disdain
like dismissing with a hand an old
beggar
it would confront you
with the assurance
of a tree offering shade

While you strut
with the challenging bombast
of a mountainous wrestler
it would greet you
with the solicitude of a mother
feeding the child with tremulous
hands

Borrowing from a nomad
a sheet for the cold night
it would face you with fortitude
with the ferocity of a lone elephant
and the deftness of a butterfly
evading your grasp

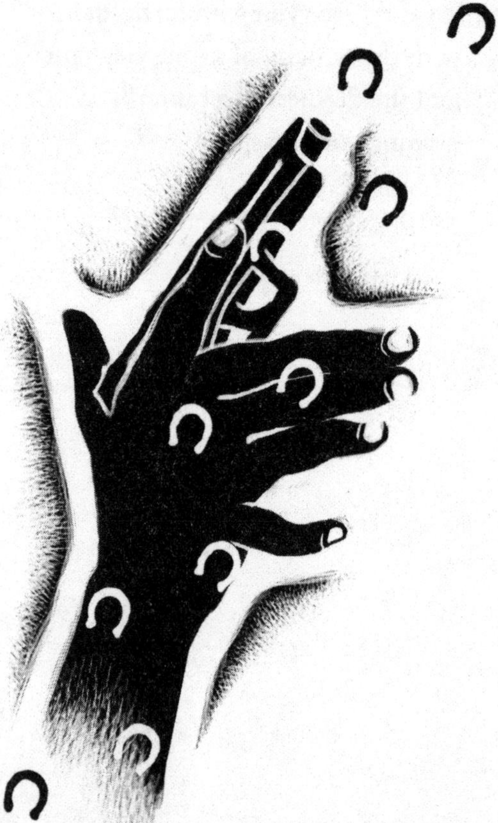

AL JANABI'S SIXTH FINGER

In Baghdad
on a March noon
with the grating and neighing
of old and decrepit horses
Time knocked at your door

With the stamp of youth still strong
the grip of dominance on the one side
the masculine arrogance
on the other
held you captive

Your body slipping
as a lump of flesh
as the sixth finger
alienated from you,
your six-year old sister watching you
with the remnant of a sweet
you had both shared
still lingering in her molar

In eerie silence they watched
the violent rape of land and woman
your mother hiding her veil
and your father at gunpoint

Inhaling the stench of rancid blood
the doddering horses panting away,
set out Time

Only witnesses

a flutter of dove wings

just a poem

* *Five American soldiers gangraped and killed 14-year old Abeer Qassim al-Janabi. This is considered to be one of the significant atrocities of American soldiers in Iraq.*

EVE'S DROP

The virgin drop
Eve tasted
was of the forbidden fruit

'After losing himself did he lose me?'
Paanchaali who waved this flag
had had the same drop

At the time of clasping Indira
This very drop
transformed into elixir for Akalikai

Maybe
beneath the board
carrying Ravana's portrait
had been Sita's first drop

After spurning love,
the eternal bowl

in Mekalai held
brimming with love:
Was it too the flow
of the same drop

Will I too be blessed with that drop?

One night
when the intense quest did not pay off
the lonely rain had let up
leaving behind a single drop
on the handle of the locked door
quenching the thirst of ages
and to charge me with life

TORTURE

My love for you
frothing in the udder
with the warmth and flavor
of freshly drawn milk
I embolden myself to share with you

The emptiness of the streets
turning silence into speech
assuring me that there is no hurdle,
I rush forward with resolve

With the enthusiasm
infected
by the wave of hand
of a little girl
returning from school
I speed with joy

This heart pulsates with the warmth

of raw meat
skinned just a while ago
and left dangling

A floating throbbing kite shows the way

I charge forward like a hound

Engulfed by the fear
that under the protracted load
your love's juices
could rot—turn rancid
oozing in your inside
I waited for a while

the flood-tide of passion
flowing out like a deep sigh

In the long run,
like a tiny food particle
stuck and grating in the molar,
all that is left

is just your memory.

OUR CHEMISTRY

Like a teardrop
Hidden inevery smile turned down

our every meeting
contained a whole range of things

Our meeting happens
with the suffocation
of a tightly strung flower string
and the sparrow
winging its way with abandon

Every time
A juxtaposing of pulsating life
and searing char—
the flutter of wings
of a bird on a canvas

TO THAT VULTURE

You stand panicked
in front of Time
which, like wings of a vulture,
snatches away your gentle smile

It stretches its arms like the barren soil
sucking away even the last drop of
water,
and waits ravenously
to gobble up even the last residue of
saliva

It hides slyly
In its ageing claws
to outrage, joy and wonder
of your youth
pure like untrodden snow

its hope fixed

on your mother's old age and dim
vision
it is savoring the sight and taste
of its prey close by

Your tiny tear drop
stays sleepless
to discern the secret path
for it to turn into a tide

As it approaches you menacingly
do reward it suitably
with no misplaced solicitude

A smile that shrouds the pain
and a pebble kissed into shape
by ageless swirl of water

THE FOREST KISS

It's a sublime
pregnant and rain-laden
evening
at the time of seeding.

While sprouting
and branching into shoots
it would heave a deep sigh
with the fatigue
of giving birth to tiny rain-drops
as watery aerial roots.

After many years
its wings grew wide
abdomen heavy
as one mighty placenta
all heavy with rain.

In its trunk carrying a nest
to collect and store love-laden dreams,
I had settled as a scale—
like the love ballad of a lonely
shepherd
reverberating in
a valley draped in silence.

The same night,
the ground yielding
and the trees softened
the warmth of my tremulous lips
would stay frozen
with the headiness
of Nagalinga flowers,

like the ancient placenta
of an Eskimo ancestor
planted at the foot of the tree

ALONE....

Dark stage settling
after rehearsal

Solitude

barrenness without make-up

Beauty

LOST

Gypsies in dazzling dresses
arrived for the temple festival

Circus clowns at wedding reception
greeting guests with effusive
handshakes

Village priests
slaughter sheep
in bloody sacrifice

The temple street at the corner
glows with gas lamps
not once but twice over.

The koothu dancers
over the years
have migrated to films
fitfully showing their faces

as old shrivelled fathers.

And
securing the old Marappachi doll
under the sarees,
and with a vanity bag in my hand

THE RIDDLE

School test for daughter:
'The presence and beauty of
butterflies.'

Presence:
Putting on myriad colours
grazing the land as momentary bliss,
darting away
as gorgeous huge rainbows,
granting liberation to fingers,
bestowing dainty residual blossom of
great love,
two wing-eyes escaping the net of eyes,
angels of love in warm chat with
breeze

So I went on

With eyes wide open

daughter quizzed:
"What do they like?
"The earthball and honey in flowers?"
"What do they not like?"
"Big thumbs, little fingers
yours and mine."

Thinking for a while she asked:

"That's all okay—

How come a lovely butterfly baby
came out of an ugly moth?"

How to solve
the riddle of beauty?

GROWTH

My first exposure to faces
more eloquent than mere words
began with Mullaikkani Nadar
—a face full of snow white beard.

How long would it take
for a tiny ant
to travel from the tip of that beard
and reach his massive moustache—
biting my nail
lost I was in childlike wonder,
a wonder that mocks at me
while in forgetful moments
I chance on his lone tomb
laced with the aroma of
white sugarmint.

In the years gone I have read

of the 'intellectual glow'
as the natural content
of a growing beard

But the goatee of
Lakshmana Teacher of Appaya
Nayakkanur
was not more frightening
than the whacking scale in his hand

Appa's prickly stubble
of two days' growth
with a fierce look
suggested anything
remotely intellectual!

STUMBLING

Maybe stumbling on a tiny word
we both could have mixed our places.

A streaky crack
Does not make a deep gorge.

After the long distance
dragged by jumping the silence,
and with marker stones in the middle
it is not possible for us both
to retrace our steps.

Perhaps when we meet
as sand slipping through our hands
as the shifting shades
beneath our trodding feet,
no chance for another embrace
without my minor bitterness in
between

Because we are inclined
to secure even the mirror
with a mirror with faded gloss
discarding the critical measures,
and parting with dignity
with a shared smile
leaves this world
beautiful for both of us.

A SHELL

O love!
Between you and me
there is only the sea
One salty teardrop of yours
settles on the shore as the sliver of
foam.

The moon above
is your Amma's frozen breastmilk;
The the sea waves,
your father's good night kisses;
and darting crabs,
your friendly playmates.

A lone shell reminds
the graffitti of prints
on your dainty palm
I secure it with care—

on the final day of judgement
standing in the long queue
changing legs to fight fatigue
and balancing the mismatch
of pangs of guilt.

ARIDITY, A BALLAD

Vanappechi the Lady of the Woods
applies Marudhaani—
not to moderate the odour of meat

With Gomathi and Pichaiamma
spurring her about
the nail-polish in flavour-free colors
available in the city

with the seven virgin 'goddesses'
each pestering her for a colour,
Pechi ventured into the city

No journey for Pechi is without
Pidaari
for engaging in friendly chat
The dust of our village is indeed sweet
but dust elsewhere is not

So saying Pidaari stole

A pair of priest's sandals
and tucked them in her armpit

To suit Pechi's bow legs
there was a plan to pilfer four

The moment she set her eyes
on the legs of greats
waving their hands
from man-sized posters,
and the dainty fingers
of the 'commercials' girls
bathed in the kisses of blinding lamps,
her hands itched for action

With the farm yard watchwoman
and the thieving Pidaari
munching the good old stories
of their journeys
neem and coconut trees as darting belles
the bazaar arrived

With the allure of a serpent with shed
skin,

the city bazaar dotted by
freebies and discounts
tore the two apart in different directions

Pidaari arrives possibly refreshed
with her booty of the day:
soft sanitary napkin for Muthumaari
who labours with washing Amma's
torn sari
to manage the month's three difficult
days.

In Pechi's string pouch
birth-control pills
for the Pandiammal of West Street
pregnant for the third time

How to deal with
the demands of the seven virgins?
Let me think it over
while returning home.
Pechi's bundles of meat
Smell of the entire city.

THE MANJANATHI TREE

Getting abraded
in your gnarled branches
I spent my childhood

Running breathless
plucking leaves from your branch
and sharing my first periods
in my teens

while a herd of sheep were munching
time
relaxing at your feet

Watching with wonder their long
beard
vaguely grappling with the gender
divide,
I spent the mystery phase
In your saree of scales

Where resided my memories
like tiny knots

stroking your massive body
extracting gum and pasting
I spent my growing years

I shared my flowering not
even with my mother
the pride of my lusty locks
reclining in your cool shade
I meandered in solitude
of my youth

Even now
in my mature youth hard to discern
I share with you and lament
my dreadful dreams

New spreading pallor,
lost friendships....
Manjanathi tree!

Languorous

At the mid-day hour

with leaves frozen still

The pain of betrayal
Is borne by your blunted thorns
Your flowers laden with toddy
are my heady secrets

Your fruits dripping with honey
know the savour of my longings

My primeval mother, Manjanathi!

Even after I turn a grand mother
stray grey sprouting on my chin
I would seek you out
to snuggle into your lap

Then
secure my shrivelled old age
in a parched leaf

Some day I would tarry and take away

the life-flower inside
like a very pregnant shepherdess

* *In Tamil Sangam Literature, Pallor (Pasalai and Themal) symbolizes suppressed libido.*

THE FOREST SMOULDERED AND DIED DOWN

On a fateful day
when hollow words and futile tears
had turned sour

before the grunt of insolent might
an ancient race
with three-millennia-long history
was forced and stripped into
nakedness

The Satan who shielded Eve's nudity
relished it

only in the tea-plantation
girdled by the sea
possibly due to the starched erection
of the uniform

Eyes and hands tied up
they bore the agony of death without
dignity
In the eerie silence
of the defenceless bodies
collapsing with head unbowed

the sky shrank in sheer torment

The land with its chest ripped apart
swore to turn barren

Have I turned into a tall tree
only to witness
this heartrending tragedy

to chime with lament of palmyra
grandma
when waves rose in resonant grief

Time filed a covenant,
conveying their last wish
to the ships not touching the floor
and the anchors still firmly planted

In the valour of fire
forest smoldered and died down

Even after this catastrophe
which no quicksand of History
can gulp down
I had to eat the next meal!

* In memory of the Eelam Tamils stripped naked, eyes and hands tied up, and shot down ruthlessly.

RAIN AND RAIN-LADEN LIFE

Difficult,
to resolve
to part with loved ones
during the rainy season
Even after slamming the door shut,
in the heaving rain would tragedy
your voice
would travel a long distance

Like rain
slipping out of the palm—
you are an expert in hiding

And wonderful Time
time is running away

DATE WITH RAIN

The rain comes unto the house
with the soft cat steps of a child
drenched and returning home late
after a spell of play in the evening
school

Your wet hands stroke my tresses
softening my little anger
and a pretense of indifference

The rain bottled up
in a spell of shyness
pours down outside

THE TASTE OF SUN

The summer
with the smile of neem
was never bitter
in the mid-day sun

after squeezing out Neem fruits
drying the seeds
converting them into coins
and savouring
sugar candies

THE LITTLE GIRL AND HER FALLEN TEETH

The words swallowed last noon
sprouted wings tonight
gathered as travel companions
other words shredded and torn
buried and hidden
in bedspreads, foot-rugs
face towels, hankies
and the pallus of sarees.

The little girl
Was burying the fallen teeth,
As the newly sprouting teeth
alludes to the old story
of the earlier fallen ones
and brought hope

Harking to an adage
not to be disdainful

of the wings coming for free
they trooped together to stage an exit

An elderly word
sounded a warning
not to give room
to a sneeze, cough or belch,
as potential hurdles to the journey,

the companion words accepted it
without objection

'Past ten at night
no hassle of traffic lights
a pleasant journey indeed,'
the young words
enthused each other

Those who disgorged accepted words
fast asleep with open mouths,
'pleasant night ahead'
they chanted
going down the steps with glee

Hearing the moaning of a word
tossed under a flower pot

'Rest for a while;
while returning I would get
some pain-relief balm'
counselled the last word
limping its way out

I have ventured out leaving behind
some more words in drains and toilets,
a middle-aged word nursed a concern

Before launching into the flight
ready to list out precautionary points,
an ancient word
buried for ages said gravely,
'No loud talking while in flight!'

A truly ancient word
with its face shrouded
rose gingerly
pulled out the wings
and prodded its ears

At the break of dawn
all the words
with plucked-out wings and
mumbling
returned to the buried spots
in evident haste

UNTITLED

When the doctor said
her womb was shaped like a question
mark
it caused her no surprise

More agitated and surprised was he
So that very evening
he published it in the newspapers
as a wonder in creation.

This has caused
embarrassment and inconvenience',
groused the husband
smoking his cigarette.
'The smoke rings
Are shaped like a question mark'
she said

A shame for the entire generation:
the birth and marital homes
were left in enigmatic dismay

An expert medical team
predicted complications in delivery
kept her under intensive watch
all the twenty-four hours

A group of visiting foreign experts
expressed an opinion
that after the delivery
the question mark could well
transform
into an exclamation-mark

A public trust gave out an assurance
to arrange for twice the leave
with maternity salary.

Glad that everyone had forgotten
the usual question of
naming the child to be born,
she was busy knitting
the standard baby sweater.

MUSICAL CHAIR

Vacant chairs tend to cause flutter

You approach a chair with a fond hope
a hanky would greet you announcing:
'Reserved'

If you charge forward
an elbow would beat you in the race

Before you wipe it and raise your head
an amply built man
would be sitting there
with an Olympic victory smile
till the a non-odorous co-passenger
arrives

it's not possible to doze off
in a vacant seat.

Chairs with the names
of retired persons
may be vacant,
but there are reserved people
to fill those seats

The chairs earmarked
for those with completed innings in
life
are mostly vacant

On the images settled as dust
can we at all sit for long
with natural trepidation

The chairs meant for granting
or seeking divine pardon
are generally vacant but not inviting

Many sacred chairs stay glittering
with none to occupy them

Their novel fashion
reminds one of quicksand

because of being vacant

A plebian can't sit on them casually

In public parks too
crow droppings get to be
ahead of us

A chair not reserved in advance
may have been made of
wood from the burial ground!

When the divine messenger
comes with his good news,
where can we find a nice chair for
him?

Some good news indeed:
The divine messenger has wings

BLESSING

The house turns new
with dismantled scaffolding
As a child enters
with no uncertainty about
where to take off the slippers
in the anklet jingle of her tender feet,
she demolishes
the severe decorum of the house
in a second

When the severity of order is
dismantled
the sofas and chairs break their languor
and spring back to life

Grazed by the saliva-soaked fingers
the belle painted on the Chinese vase
breaks into a momentary smile
The marble floor

hungering for the blessing of muck
anointed by the babe's lukewarm piss
sheds its inertia and gets sensitized

A piece of glass
from the pickle jar broken
shares with glee
its charming toothless smile
with the other smithereens

When the baby jumps
from one shoulder to the other
the swing waits impatiently
to swing its legs in unison.

With the infant being carried
without the feet touching the floor
the stairs look at herlongingly
drawing mild jeer from the swing

The railing of the staircase
anointed by saliva-smeared hand

Wrapping the foot rug as waist-towel,
tossing the laundered hankies

in the trash can,
she feeds the fish in the fish-tank
with rules turned topsy-turvy

Weary of feeling trapped
in the aneamic orderliness
of the decorative cabinet,
the curious lost in prayer that the baby
should not fall asleep out of fatigue

The paintings on the wall
having observed the display of revolt
turn themselves upside down
and deck themselves in a great hurry

The accumulated cobwebs
Of lifeless formal words
wiped clean
by a solitary meaningless sound.

In the yard
only the Buddha in deep meditation
disappeared
the moment the infant moved away

GENERATION

She
like burning sands of the desert
I
like the rain-soaked earthen floor

The third one
likethe fresh flood surging out of a
sluice

We were all born
in some month in one year
on a none too unusual day

The birds aren't going to return,
She said
But they are sure return to feed the
young ones
I said
Thrill is the essence of flight,

said the third.

Nights are endearing
declared she,
Sunset is alluring for me
The mystique attracts me,
asserted the third.

Only questions
not demanding answers
are permitted, said she.
I believe in the
possibilities of discussion.
The third is inclined towards
the assertiveness of authority

Raw vegetables fruits—
her choice
Well-cooked hot food—
my taste.
'Rare' meat with a trace of blood—
the preference of the third

The majesty of fasting is best

for her.
Savouring good digestion, for me.
Size Zero of Anorexia,
For the third.

Easy style in dress, her penchant.
Tradition and modernity
mingling as warp and woof is my
choice.
Indeterminate nudity suits the third.

Universe was her abode.
Comfortable home
washed by breeze and light
is what I prefer
A house is a superfluous luxury
is the reckoning of the third.

For her,
language is prayer.
For me
the breath of life
determined by feelings and needs.
For the third

the sound of ribaldry

All born, traversed and merged
In this ocean
which drop is mine?

IT WAS SUNSET TIME

God has stolen the night from me
And filed a complaint

Satan agreed to negotiate
a settlement

'Why is night more essential than day?
Let him explain Clearly
We will then think about returning it'

'Night strips the day's man naked,
changes his form,
it is then he needs badly
my protection and monitoring',
argued God.

'God has captured day-time
in the fear of sin,
only during night

can one lean on a shoulder
and seek refuge
My task is to
provides help
to children and weak elders',
argued Satan.

A plebian traveller
found it needless
for two sorcerers
to be meddling in his privacy.

'As water in the ocean,
as fish in the hook,
only I provide
life-support to man',
said God
with a disarming smile

At that point
Satan's noose gripped his neck.
'It is flagrant midday aggression.
Satan interfering
With my authority',

God remonstrated.

'Transgression is my norm
Watching fun is God's habit.'
Satan concluded the conversation.

With God at the dead man's feet
Satan beside his head
There was relief at last

It was sunset

AN ENCOUNTER

I chanced upon a word
White attempting suicide

For me to prepare a lecture,
And for the word to see liberation,
we chose a discreet corner

Suicide is a private affair
But as I can't be a witness to a suicide
I enquired Reason

Just a movement of the mouth
to speed up its decision

But the word demanded
That the discussion be in a sign
language

When I tried

I found I was totally defenceless.
'It's kindness I seek
it's ever so important.
Don't forsake me

As I took courage to speak,
in a fit of rage,
it started strangling itself
and got ready to die
In keeping with a court's formality
I hurled the usual question,
'Do you have any last wish?'

'Before I commit suicide,
Let the misfortune of meeting
the person who instigated it
happen to any other word,'
said the word.

ARUGAN

I discovered you
on the bank of my Kanmaai pond
as the tail of a Sempothu bird
I couldn't help telling this
to Karuppan of broken sickle
I recall his eyebrows
arching into a smile

I observed a Black Babul tree
shaking vigorously with a mock smile.
Your form got imprinted in my mind
as the footprint of a peacock.
Defying description in words,
the black earth
made up for my inadequacy
with its own deft lines

The strapping palmyra friends
fanned themselves

with my sigh of delight
at touching a heady height.
For its part
the Pirandai plant swathed in thorns
shed a solitary thorn
and released a charming smile
On hearing your name
a sturdy thorn of a black babul tree
gave out an obstinate grunt
like a child[1] weeping
The drumstick tree
dropped a couple of pieces
broke into convulsive laughter,
showering a bunch of
tiny yellow flowers.
Across the stream
you may well be standing
removing the Nerunji thorns
strewn on my path.

My Arugan!
After time and space
have become our own
why worry about place and distance?

If for the tiny Sempothu
two steps to tread
and an Ilandai berry to taste
are enough
we too live happily
in this wide world

MY DEATH

As a piece of meat
grabbed by the time-vulture
I am buried
in the dark depths of a dense forest
The woods are not the exclusive home
of birds returning to their nests
and for the fledglings left alone

The silence hounded by words
has congealed as the puss
out of the gash on the wounded
animal.
As the Eesal termites' swarming
after a downpour,
I am inundated with waves of memory
and ravenous hunger
so impatient as to devour its own
breath

Praying for the
freedom from sobbing,
anguish is on its knees
Only the right hand is trying to relieve
the pain of left shoulder
My nostril is buried in the sand
praying for mother's milk.

The earth that consumes
the earth that yielded you
and the ancestors,
the earth that digests me
with the juice of the hills and woods
and the aroma of your kiss

The woods are not the preserve
of only the little ones left alone
but also belongs to the fireflies
which live for one glorious moment.

The mind-serpent
discards its skin of darkness
and grows lighter
The woods, not meant

only for fireflies with a
fleeting spark-life,
also belongs to butterflies
with sprouted wings

WHAT?

Is night only darkness?
Sprucing the passion of love
and stroking the body-feather
the seven-hued rainbow;
savouring with closed eyes
when infant' lips suck breast;

melody-soaked flute
when the moon
seeps through the inner garment
and loosens it

It is a serpent
in eye-drooping stupor
followed by a raised hood
when the little finger
touches the tiny ant
climbing the rim of the cot
it's a forest of countless species

A drop of rain dripping into the house
and clearing the muck of the morning;
mother's bosom
pulsating with plentiful milk;
When dream grabs the moments
tailed by memory
it is the weightless bodies
of my ancestors

Is the night
shrouding the rehearsal for light
mere darkness?

THE OTHER SIDE

The poem
with maximum translation:
the moon

A leprous patch for a refugee

a silver milk bowl for the lucky

in the luxury of his homeland:
the moon

For the aggressor her nectar,
for the oppressed her pure venom

What trickles through
my coconut fronds
is the same moon
common to one and all.

In the stomach without hunger
in my home land
over my thatched roof
kindling passion within me

This very Moon
could be a nameless anguish
of a shamed prostitute
in a land devastated
by an earthqua

The moon that shrinks or expands
inside men's palms
or filling the sky real
Caught in a dread
that even on a New Moon night
a poem may emerge
about the moon

THE SHADOW

It was the street-corner neem tree
which immediately shared with me
my intense grief
of the loss of a very dear friend.

On that day
it was buried in heavy silence
unmindful ofeven the cawing of a
crow

When I lingered in its shade
it gave me the look of a garden lizard.
'You know my pain' I said
'This is exactly
what your girl friend would tell me
this evening
as she would pass by,' it said.
I tightly hugged it.

A crow, after cawing away
the shadow of my grief
disappeared

TO EACH UNTO HERSELF

The black palmyra down in the
ground,
like Ekalaivan's finger cut off
On that I was sitting
like an empty toddy pot
after the brew has been exhausted
With the stench of cheroot
laced with the aroma of toddy
by the side was, Vanappechi

Spreading a part of the saree
Seelaikkaari was warding off
the fury of burning sand

With the juice trickling
down to the elbow,
savouring the palmyra fruit

With laughter uncontrollable

the seven virgins
were decking their eyes
with the black grease from the cart

One of them said:
"The guys run a mile
away from the stench
of the neem oil in our head."
No wonder our virginity will last
For ever

Polishing off the palmyra fruit
Raakkaachi threw the fruit on her
and says:
"They are possibly better than
the bastards who leave half way."
Looking at her swelling breasts
bursting through her blouse
Seelaikkaari had this to say:
"Only in the world shorn of them
would beauty stay steadfast."
Immersed in the heat of the cheroot,
Vanappechi continued:
"The island across the shore

apparently is full of widows
like the sprinkling of sesame seeds
afte all the paraphernalia
of the Ayyanar temple festival
including the ritual slaughter……
Whether it a she, he or they
if a nondescript birth without womb
and breasts
Perhaps Koneswari and Pennamperi
can be born there without fear
Like in love, no age in war too
And in widowhood"

I tossed away
the blank sheets I had gathered
to write poems
Let the urchins of the palmyra waste
use it to wipe their bums!

Koneswari, Pennamberi: In the eighties these two Tamil girls were raped by Sri Lankan soldiers and ruthlessly slaughtered.

HANDSHAKE AND LOUDSPEAKERS

You observe only the
spoken word
ignoring with disdain
the language
of the eyes, earlobes and fingers

Do you at all know
the pumpkin flower
planted in the Markazhi kolam
in the opposite yard
is a heart!

THE THROB OF SILENCE

In the dark cave of silence
when your gentle smile
attempts to escape through a crevice
as a tiny streak of light,
your lone word blocks the way
as a huge rock.

ODE TO SOFTWARE

The 'beep' sounds announce
the short messages
The notes exchanged all night
stay wiped out in your chat realm
and the moisture of kisses
have dried up
Your inbox brimming with
smile—likes and thanks
Like a stallion itching for the race,
your cell phone.
With so many 'soft' notes
eagerly lingering
how come you're still asleep,
O Software girl!

GREETING MORROW

Savoured by time
A delicious sweet, your youth
Look, withering makes you desiccated.
Before you open the front door
the echo of your smile
is like the sticker tilak on the mirror.
Your hands that had challenged
Your sturdy shoulders
with the fatigue of bearing
the weight of your nails-
a puzzle for me

Your tongue only licks
the puss of mighty grief
Your face is buried in the termite
anthill
with the dismay of a child
that has lost its way

It appears to bejust yesterday when,
from your eyes tingling with youth,
you shared drops dripping with grace

From your palm brimming with
pollen
you lavished love on me
like a Shenbaga flower.
From your shoulders
offering shelter to many birds

you bestowed on me
a slice of your warmth:

a luscious fig fruit

On a fine day
in a world without clocks and
calendars
I plant a kiss on your forehead
and return
May we carry the tomorrow
Without yesterday's taints

A NEW ANGLE

The palmyra trees in a state of bliss
immersed in a dream
of inebriated dark crows mating
The sandy wastes in Theri woods
luxuriate in the marks of
the snail's love games.
The Surai creepers intertwining
passionately
the moon swells her breasts
and flowers in star nipples
The singed taste of palmyra root
scales the fence
like Akalikai's passion.

The dry dung cakes
carrying the beehives of unshared
kisses
turn placid and drop off

Live cinders of the clay oven
on the unloading of the rice pot,
the tiny palmyra strands
serving as residual fuel feed
and bestows pulsations on the night

With palmyra grove bathed in aroma
Pechi treading the sandy stretch
walks with unexpressed passion
like the kitchen discharge
silently traversing the backyard

A palm swirls in her hand
full of great formidable grief
These woods
Exist not for the affluent
with wealth bursting at its seams
but for Sickle Karuppans.

GENITAL BLOOD

Empty pots reeking of toddy
at a time of residual post-coital rest,
Pechi was tidying tobacco strands for a
cheroot

At the rim of the weary upturned
toddy pots
the smile of stupor frozen

Tiny ants were tottering
savouring the crumbs from Pechi's
mouth
on tossing the leftovers of
the cleaned palymra reeds

Well-made cheroots
waiting for the touch of Pechi's thick
lips.

Muthalamma Picked up a dot
from the searing heat of mid-day
and lit it up
Sniffing the acid stench of Vinodhini,
moaned Sokkaathamma

Smelling Nirbaya's private sore
started singing Oppari
Seelaikkaari Amma,
Pidaari wailed a pilaakkanam piece
Sangeetha's school uniform
tattered by the impact of thorny bush
was flying halfmast.

Muthumari in the grip of fright
that the cheroot has transformed
into an iron rod shafted
into a female genital

The Border Kali yelled:
a beast was seen at the tip of
Kanmaai Karuppan's sickle.

The virgins panted away shouting

that the sullied clothes
which had borne abdominal pains
has been burnt down with black babul
woods.
Raakkaachi mumbled hesitantly:
the black-cloth of the Lord of Justice
has been dabbed with an intoxicant
Pechi spat out
The burnt out cheroot cinder

Entire palmyra woods
we're bathed in genital blood

In the eyes of Karuppan
sobbing away kneeling
the Kanmaai started yelling

* *This poem weaves into its fabric two horrible cases of gang rape and sexual assault (Nirbhaya and Sangeeta) which evoked massive moral outrage.*

UNTITLED

No heart to shake away
the sun clasping my legs
I wrapped him on
as in a passionate embrace
Love
pours out as sweat

EVOLUTIONARY CHANGE

The house has adopted Amma
for its exclusive use.
She settles with a smile the quarrel
about the shirt not properly folded
but no one notices the
wrinkle on her face
till the food loses its taste and warmth
her weak moan and exhaustion
Is not even acknowledged.

Even when she drops as dried
shrivelled leaf
they find it easy to blame
her lack of responsibility,
but while popping up prescribed pills,
Amma doesn't forget to advise them
against cold water bath.

When she attempts

to become one for herself too
it was too late.
I have already started
becoming a mother

HOPE ENDURING

The tree is blossoming
spreading its wings
dotted with bird droppings

Its leaves are waiting for a downpour
as a cleansing benefactor.
Then, how will this tiny nest escape?

With the blessing
that the weak can
vanquish the strong,
the mother bird
lands with its long wing

with the hues of Aram.

RAIN FINDS ITS LEVEL

With a charming wink
the hands love in our palm.
The passion's lily sprouts branches
through the crevices of desire's fingers
This night secures the seed of kindness
blossoming even in old age
in the kiss on the forehead
at the end of a union.

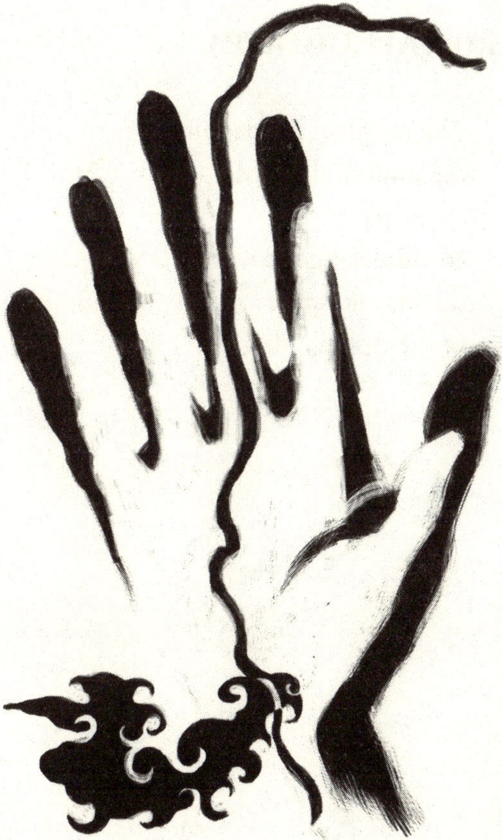

FROM APPA TO APPA

The moment of snapping
the umbilical chord,
in the palm
encountering the world
the first skyspace
of the Appas.

NOT MUCH, O WORTHIES!

From time immemorial
they had stood up
five feet away from me.
They moved away
that my shadow
is a polluting presence.
They had fattened
consuming as tears
my salt and sweat

They had brought down to our hip
our shoulder towel in a trice
and to haul it up again
it took us generations ten

Our parai is not a bit inferior
to Veena Saraswathi had given them
it is given only to this generation
to establish this.

Like the sword of Democles
they planted their 'purity'
in our living rooms

We have been
observing all this.

Surreptitiously
They stole pages from our books
and inserted their history

Have been reading it

Ever so silently
they're now entering
our kitchen.

Blunting our tastebuds
by anointing with ghee,
urge us to wash and purify
our kitchen
In our belch
garnished with blood-tinted meat,
they discern and complain about

the stench of Viduthalai.

We keep
observing it.

Today
perched on the kitchen chimney
they sniff around.

Tomorrow....
May enter even our bedrooms
claiming to purify our private world
spreading incense there too.

Would we keep
observing then too?

Okay
What would you do?
One word to those suggesting
the submission of a Manu (petition)
to them.

Let us change places

Henceforth
why not they submit
memorandum to us?

Worthies!
Not much distance
between 'Manu' the
memorandum
and 'Manu' the 'law giver'
—A mere one hundred years!

* *Manu in Tamil means Memorandum. Manu also refers to the ancient Hindu law giver whose script tends to advocate differential moral and legal norms on community lines.*

DEFEAT

The pen opens with the gusto
of a bloodhound.
Closes sometimes
with the feeble moan
of a sick old woman—
when poetry lingers
as granular residue
between the emotional orgasm
and the obstinate filter of words.

THE GREAT ARRIVAL

Ever since dawn
the house was in a flutter

A desire long ago
the dream of a computer
would be within reach
before the evening

A call from the dealer
gave the good tidings.

The next moment
like a waterfall in abandon
the house reverberated with joy.
As if waiting for a favourite guest
the yard and the verandah
decked themselves up
The whole tribe was eager and ecstatic
to greet a newborn.

Only two bedrooms
Were making room by juggling
beyond question
Living room too was
ruled out as unsuitable.

To make room in the verandah
north corner near window
the home for the computer,
the die was cast.

The old curtain was parted;
the windows—dusted
From the frame fell the curtains
and also
a fluffy velvety soft fibre nest.

I held it in my hand
with the memory
of my dear Appa's charming story
about the squirrel's lines

Exactly at that moment
the joy of the computer's arrival
disappeared totally

GLOSSARY

Akalikai: A character in Ramayana epic. Wife of a sage, she succumbs to the viles of Indra and is cursed by her husband to be turned into stone. She is eventually redeemed when the dust from Rama's feet settles on her. A nucleus for a number of creative weaving of stories in modern Tamil literature.

Amma: Mother

Appa: Father

Aram: A Tamil term which encompasses all the noble ethical and behavioural norms in life.

Beedi: Processed tobacco rolled up in a dry tendu leaf for smoking.

Chembu: A small vessel with a narrow neck for carrying water, milk etc.

Eesal: A form of winged termite.

Kanmaai: Small lake or irrigation tank.

Kolam: Decorative design drawn on floor, etc., with powder or flour or flour-paste.

Koothu: A form of folk theatre with song, dialogue and movements, enacting stories from mythology.

Marappachi: Wooden doll for little girls.

Marudhaani: Leaves of the plant henna crushed and used as dye applied on the palms and nails.

Nerunji: A small-sized plant hugging the ground and consisting of thorns and small yellow flowers.

Oppaari: Lamentation on the death of a person, consisting of wailing and sorrowful singing.

Paanchaali: A character in the Mahabaratha epic. The consort of the five Pandava princes.

Parai: A large round drum usually associated with funeral procession. In recent times, it has come to symbolize Dalit resurgence.

Pilaakkanam: Lament for the dead in the form of a mournful songs.

Pirandai: Square-stalked vine; used as an input in native medicine.

Pongal: Votive offering of rice, the cooking of which is done in the temple precinct; agricultural festival celebrated on the first day of the Tamil month 'Thai', when rice cooked with jiggery or with salt is offered to the Sun god.

Thinnai: Raised platform on which people sit, usually in the verandah or on either side of the front door of the house.

Tilak: An ornamental mark on the forehead (of women)

Viduthalai: A newspaper founded by the patriarch of the Dravidian moment Periyar E.V.Ramasamy. Continuing to this day, it stands for iconoclastic atheism and social equality.

* *The Translator acknowledges with gratitude the support provided by CreA's contemporary Tamil Dictionary in constructing this Glossary.*

ABOUT THE TRANSLATOR

A renowned name in the field of literary translation, the late **Dr KS Subramanian** has translated over 40 Tamil literary works into English. These include novels, novellas, collection of short stories and anthologies of poetry. He has also translated a large number of collected essays and biographical and autobiographical works. His translations have been published by the Sahitya Akademi, Macmillan, Katha, East-West Books, Westland, Tamil University, International Institute of Tamil Studies, Central Institute of Indian Languages and others.

He has received several awards for his translations, including the 'Outstanding Translator Award' by the Government of Tamil Nadu, 'Kalaignar – BAPASI' Award and the 'Nalli – Thisai Ettum' Translation Award.

Dr Subramanian was the compiling editor of *Jayakanthan Reader* and presented numerous papers on eminent creative writers of Tamil such as Subramania Bharathi, Na Pichamurthy, La Sa Ramamirtham, Thi Janakiraman among others. Ten volumes of his Tamil articles and papers have been published covering literary, social and developmental themes.

A former member of the Jury for Sahitya Akademi awards for Tamil and Translation, Dr KS Subramanian was also a trustee of MOZHI, a resource centre for Tamil language and culture.